4|08

TORNADOES

Earth's Power

David and Patricia Armentrout

Rourke
Publishing LLC
Vero Beach, Florida 32964

www.rourkepublishing.com

PHOTO CREDITS: Pgs 5, 10, 13, 17, 25 ©Weatherpix Stock Images; Title pg ©Gregory Runyan; Pg 6 inset ©Rod Renolds; Pgs 9 inset, 13 inset, 15 courtesy of NOAA/Department of Commerce; Pgs 6, 9, 14, 17 inset, 18, 21, 21 inset, 25 inset, 29 courtesy of FEMA; Pg 22 courtesy of Marvin Nauman/FEMA; Cover, pg 18 inset ©Noel Clark; Pg 26 courtesy of the Department of Defense

Title page: A developing thundercloud in Oklahoma.

Editor: Robert Stengard-Olliges

Cover and page design by Nicola Stratford

Library of Congress Cataloging-in-Publication Data

Armentrout, David, 1962-
  Tornadoes / David and Patricia Armentrout.
     p. cm. -- (Earth's power)
  Includes bibliographical references and index.
  ISBN 1-60044-233-1 (hardcover)
  ISBN 978-1-60044-342-8 (paperback)
  1. Tornadoes--Juvenile literature. I. Armentrout, Patricia, 1960- II.
Title. III. Series: Armentrout, David, 1962- Earth's power.
QC955.2.A76 2007
551.55'3--dc22

                          2006011220

Printed in the USA

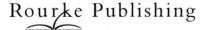

Rourke Publishing

www.rourkepublishing.com – sales@rourkepublishing.com
Post Office Box 3328, Vero Beach, FL 32964

TABLE OF CONTENTS

TORNADO

A tornado is the most violent windstorm on earth. Tornadoes can form anywhere, but most occur in the United States. Severe tornadoes are more common in the central plains; an area often referred to as Tornado Alley.

A tornado is a rotating column of air that extends from a cloud to the ground. A tornado is usually visible as a **funnel cloud**, but not always. A funnel cloud is a rotating column of air made up of water droplets. A funnel cloud is a tornado only if it touches the ground.

On average, 1,200 tornadoes are reported yearly in the U.S.

Tornadoes may be beautiful to look at, but can be extremely dangerous.

A dark supercell thunderstorm approaches.

Twisted metal is all that is left of this mobile home after a tornado, spawned from hurricane Jeanne, struck South Carolina in 2004.

WHAT MAKES A TORNADO?

When warm, moist air rises rapidly and meets cool, dry air it creates an unstable environment. Unstable air masses can produce thunderstorms. Some severe thunderstorms can produce tornadoes.

Thunderstorms in different stages of development can merge forming a multicell storm. A line of multicell storms, called a squall line, can sometimes produce a tornado. Most violent tornadoes, though, form from very large, organized thunderstorms called **supercells**.

Tornadoes can occur any time of the year. Peak tornado season in the U.S. is spring and summer. Most tornadoes form in the late afternoon or evening hours.

7

SUPERCELL THUNDERSTORMS

A supercell is the most dangerous kind of thunderstorm. Supercells can produce lightning, heavy rains, flash flooding, **hail**, strong straight-line winds, and tornadoes.

All thunderstorms have an **updraft**—a current of rising air. A supercell thunderstorm has a rotating updraft called a **mesocyclone**. Mesocyclone is a term **meteorologists** use to describe how a rotating updraft looks on a **radar** screen. A mesocyclone can stretch two to six miles across. Scientists believe most strong and violent tornadoes form from a mesocyclone.

Lightning is the most dangerous part of a thunderstorm. It kills more people each year than tornadoes.

A flash flood in West Virginia left a thick layer of silt after the water receded.

Dirt and debris swirl violently around this large
tornado near Manchester, South Dakota

TRACKING A STORM

Meteorologists use radar to track thunderstorms. Weather radar sends out radio waves from an antenna. The waves bounce off objects in the air, such as raindrops or ice crystals. The objects cause some waves to reflect, or echo, back to the antenna. The time it takes an antenna to receive an echo determines the distance of the object. Computers convert the echoes into data and display them on a radar screen.

1925 Tri-State Tornado:

The single most deadly tornado killed an estimated 695 people as it moved across parts of Missouri, Illinois, and Indiana on March 18, 1925. The twister traveled 219 miles at an average speed of 62 miles an hour.

DOPPLER RADAR

One of the most important tools a meteorologist uses is Doppler radar. Doppler radar can tell a forecaster a great deal about the structure of a thunderstorm. Doppler radar determines location of precipitation, but also measures the speed and direction in which the precipitation is moving. Doppler radar is sensitive enough to show the direction and speed of wind blowing around precipitation. If intense wind circulation is seen on radar, the possibility of a tornado exists.

1974 April 3-4 Super Outbreak:

Within 16 hours, 147 tornadoes hit 13 states, killing 310 people and injuring more than 5,000. It is the deadliest outbreak in U.S. history. The most notable tornado in the outbreak hit Xenia, Ohio. It killed 34 people and destroyed half the town.

Most tornadoes last only a few minutes.

Mobile Doppler radar scans an approaching supercell thunderstorm.

13

An official with the Federal Emergency Management Agency (FEMA) monitors a tornado outbreak.

STORM PREDICTION

The Storm Prediction Center (SPC) is headquartered in Norman, Oklahoma. Scientists at the center monitor and forecast severe weather, and issue thunderstorm and tornado watches. A watch is issued when conditions are right for the formation of severe thunderstorms or tornadoes.

The SPC works with the National Weather Service (NWS). The NWS has more than 120 offices across the country. A local office will issue a tornado warning if a tornado has been seen in an area, or one has been indicated on radar.

STORM SPOTTERS AND CHASERS

Storm spotters are often the first lines of defense against deadly tornadoes. They can be volunteers or paid public officials like the police. They monitor stormy skies looking for visual clues that can lead to tornado development. They send information to local weather service offices.

Storm chasers usually "chase" as a hobby because they find it thrilling. Some storm chasers are meteorologists conducting research. Others may be making a living photographing and filming tornadoes.

The 1999 Great Plains tornado outbreak left thousands homeless.

A storm chaser gets a little too close for comfort.

A classic white twister in Kansas.

MOTHER LIBERTY CME CHURCH

4D 40

ecember 15, 1870, in Jackson, the Colored
odist Episcopal Church was organized
e General Conference of the Methodist
pal Church South. The first official
Church, "Mother Liberty," which stood one
west, was razed by fire in the late
In 1893 the church was relocated to

A historic church in Jackson, Tennessee was heavily damaged by an F4 tornado in 2003.

TORNADO FAST FACTS

Tornadoes come in many colors, shapes and sizes. Some are gray, white, or even a pale shade of blue. Others are difficult to see until they pick up dirt or other debris, taking on the color of the soil, like brownish-red, or black.

Tornadoes often resemble a long, thin tube sweeping across the sky. Some have a classic funnel shape—wide at the top and narrow at the bottom. Still, other tornadoes are as wide as they are tall, and are hard to tell apart from their parent storm cloud.

2003 May:
In all, 543 tornadoes were recorded in May of 2003. The most in any month since record keeping began in 1950.

2004 May 22
Hallam, Nebraska
Outbreak:

More than 20 tornadoes broke out in Nebraska. The most damaging hit the small town of Hallam, population 276. It destroyed most of the buildings and caused one death. The tornado goes on record for being the widest—it caused a two and a half mile-wide damage path.

About 69 percent of all tornadoes are classified as weak, with winds of 110 miles an hour or less. Twenty-nine percent are strong, with winds ranging from 110-205 miles an hour. Only about two percent of all tornadoes are violent storms with winds greater than 205 miles an hour.

Weak tornadoes typically last up to ten minutes. Strong tornadoes can last up to 20 minutes. Violent tornadoes can exceed an hour, and are responsible for 70 percent of all tornado deaths.

Some residents of Hallam, Nebraska had little left to salvage.

Corn is removed from silos destroyed by a tornado that struck Hallam, Nebraska.

Tornado damage is surveyed in South Carolina.

ESTIMATING DAMAGE

The Fujita Scale estimates a tornado's wind speed by the damage it caused to man-made structures. Meteorologist Ted Fujita developed it in 1971. An Enhanced F-scale (EF scale) is now used.

The Enhanced F-scale is based on engineering guidelines for 28 different types of structures, including barns, mobile homes, brick buildings, shopping malls, and transmission towers. Surveyors access the damage in relation to wind measurements taken in the area. The tornado is then given an EF-rating based on the data.

Below is a wind rating comparison between the original Fujita Scale and the Enhanced Fujita Scale.

F-Scale	Fastest 1/4 mile wind speeds, mph	Enhanced F-Scale	3-Second Gust Speed, mph
F0	< 73	F0	65-85
F1	73-112	F1	86-110
F2	113-157	F2	111-135
F3	158-207	F3	136-165
F4	208-260	F4	166-200
F5	261-318	F5	> 200

An F3 tornado killed two people and left a 17.5 mile-long path of destruction in Maryland.

An awesome sight as a tornado rips through hay bales on a Kansas farm.

A military helicopter keeps a close watch on a nearby waterspout.

WATERSPOUTS

A tornado that forms over water is called a **waterspout**. Waterspouts can form over oceans, bays, and even lakes. Many form along the Florida coast, particularly in the Keys.

Most waterspouts do not form from a supercell. They are considered weak tornadoes, called fair weather waterspouts. However, they can overturn small boats or seriously damage structures if they hit land. A waterspout is a tornado, but it will not be recorded as one unless it hits land.

CONTINUED

RESEARCH

Meteorologists still cannot predict exactly which storms will spawn tornadoes, or where they will strike. That is why scientists continue to study them at the National Severe Storms Laboratory in Oklahoma. New Doppler radar systems have enabled forecasters to increase advance-warning time. Advance warning gives people time to move to safe shelter. Improved warning times has decreased the number of injuries and has saved lives.

Taking *Shelter* From The Storm

Building a SAFE ROOM Inside Your Home

The purpose of a safe room is to provide a space where you and your family can survive a tornado or hurricane with little or no injury.

There are several possible locations in your house for a safe room, but regardless of where you build it, your safe room must be able to remain standing through high winds, even if your house is severely damaged.

Did You Know...

Almost every state in the U.S. is subject to extreme windstorms and the serious threat these events pose to buildings and their occupants.

FEMA, in cooperation with the Wind Engineering Research Center of Texas Tech University, has developed designs for wind shelters, or "safe rooms", that homeowners can build inside their houses. These shelters are designed to provide protection from the forces of extreme winds as high as 250 mph, including the impact of windborne debris.

ARE YOU READY?

A FEMA official reviews a storm safety display.

GLOSSARY

funnel cloud (FUHN uhl KLOUD) — a funnel-shaped cloud with a rotating column of air that extends down from the base of a cloud

hail (HAYL) — balls or irregular pieces of ice, five millimeters or more in diameter, that usually form in thunderstorm clouds

mesocyclone (MEH zoe SY klone) — an area of vertical wind rotation found in supercell thunderstorms

meteorologist (MEE tee ur OL oh jist) — people who study the atmosphere which causes weather conditions

radar (RAY dar) — **RA**dio **D**etection **A**nd **R**anging; an electronic instrument used to detect, determine the distance of, and map objects

supercells (SOO per selz) — the strongest type of thunderstorm

updraft (UHP draft) — air with vertical motion that if combined with moisture can form a cloud that may develop into a thunderstorm

waterspout (WAW ter spout) — a tornado that forms over water

FURTHER READING

Osborne, Will and Mary Pope. *Twisters and other Terrible Storms.* Scholastic, 2003.

Challoner, Jack. *Hurricane & Tornado.* Dorling Kindersley, 2004.

White, Matt. *Storm Chasers: On the Trail of Deadly Tornadoes.* Capstone Press, 2003.

WEBSITES TO VISIT

National Weather Service
www.nws.noaa.gov

FEMA For Kids
www.fwma.gov/kids/tornado.htm

Weather Wiz Kids
www.weatherwizkids.com/index.htm

INDEX

ABOUT THE AUTHORS

David and Patricia Armentrout have written many nonfiction books for young readers. They have had several books published for primary school reading. The Armentrouts live in Cincinnati, Ohio, with their two children.